Listening to Dialogues on Social Issues

社会的な問題についての会話リスニング15章

by
James M. Vardaman
Kaoru Noji

TSURUMI SHOTEN

はじめに

　本書の各章は社会的な問題についての男性と女性の二人の会話文を中心にして構成されています。全15章の各トピックの内容は日本であるいは世界で問題になっているものばかりですので、興味をもって会話を聴くことができることと思います。

　会話中心のテキストは日常の簡単な挨拶や外国旅行の英会話といったものも多いのですが、本書の会話の内容や使われている表現やその話し方は大学生が聞いたり話したりするのにふさわしいものとなっています。

　本書は会話が主体のテキストですが、会話そのものはDictation用の部分を除き印刷されていますので、文字によっても会話の内容を確認することが出来ます。会話で聴くと理解するのが内容的に難しいと思っても、Dictationの解答を記入した後ですべての内容を文字で確認することが出来ます。

　本書は学生のみなさんの英語力の向上を図ることを第一の目的として書かれたものです。そのため、会話を聴くことによって聴解力と表現力がつくようにDictationを主体とした聴解力向上のための練習問題や会話に出てきた使用頻度の高い表現を覚えるための例文やその応用問題などを配しています。ただ、聴解力と表現力は表裏の関係にあると言ってもよく、聴解力が高まれば自然と表現力も身につくものですので、音声を何度でも繰り返し聴く努力をすることはとても大切なことだと思います。逆に、知らない単語や表現の聞き取りは難しいと言えるかもしれません。そのためにはテキストを読むことが役にたちます。

　本書が学生のみなさんの英語コミュニケーション能力の向上と社会的な問題への関心をさらに呼び起こすことに役立つことが出来ればと願ってやみません。

2017年11月

James M. Vardaman

野地　薫

各章の構成と使用法

冒頭の短い紹介文で Dialogue の内容の背景を把握します。

Dialogue
- 全章が男女二人の会話になっています。
- Dictation をする部分は英語に対応した日本語が印刷されています。
- 会話は全体を 3 つのブロックに分けてあります。

Try!
1. Dictation
- 会話で日本語で印刷されている部分の英語がもう一度ややゆっくりと話されるので書きとる練習をします。Dictation 部分は 5 か所から 6 か所となっています。

2. Vocabulary in Dictation
- Dictation の文中にある表現を覚えるための例文が各 3 つあり、3 つ目の文は日本語になっているので自分で英語にして英訳例の音声と比較します。

3. Comprehension Check
- Dialogue のそれぞれのブロックの内容について述べた文を読んでその文の内容が T か F かを答える問題です。

Try more!
- 各章のトピックに関連したややくだけた内容の男女の短めの会話を聴きます。Partial Dictation となっているので空欄を埋めます。

Questions for Discussion
- 各トピックに関連して、学習者自身の意見や感想、知識を尋ねる質問です。

CONTENTS

Chapter 1	**Civilian Drones**..2	
	ドローン利用法	
Chapter 2	**Reading While Young**..6	
	青春と読書	
Chapter 3	**Intelligent Assistance**.....................................10	
	AI より IA で	
Chapter 4	**Keeping It Clean**..14	
	リサイクルの大切さ	
Chapter 5	**Manners in Public**...18	
	日本的美徳	
Chapter 6	**Which News Is Fake?**......................................22	
	フェイクの見極め	
Chapter 7	**Food Self-sufficiency**.....................................26	
	回復しない食料自給率	
Chapter 8	**Whose Fish?**..30	
	やせるサンマ	
Chapter 9	**English: Necessary or Not?**...........................34	
	英語必修論	
Chapter 10	**Career Education**..38	
	キャリア教育	
Chapter 11	**Hours Worked**..42	
	過重労働	
Chapter 12	**Gender Equality**..46	
	ジェンダー・ギャップ	
Chapter 13	**Where Does the Stress Come From?**............50	
	ストレスはどこから	
Chapter 14	**The Age of Childlessness**..............................54	
	少子化時代の覚悟	
Chapter 15	**Less Romance in Japan**.................................58	
	ロマン不在時代？	

١

Listening to Dialogues on Social Issues

★★★★★★★★★★

社会的な問題についての会話リスニング 15 章

Chapter 1 Civilian Drones

ドローン利用法

ドローン (drone) とはミツバチの雄バチの意味もあり、のらくら者のことをいう場合もある。しかし、現代の空飛ぶドローンはのらくら者どころではない。ドローンがからむ人騒がせな事件もあって、その利用法をめぐっては議論もある。しかし、現実となっている様ざまな平和的な利用法についてはその将来性にも多くのことが期待されるようになっている。

Dialogue

まず会話を聴きましょう。日本語になっている部分の英語は印刷されていません。 2–4

 2

A: Did you hear about the foreign visitor who operated a drone over the pedestrians on Ginza Dori one weekend? The police caught him. He told them he just wanted to take videos of the famous area.

B: That seems like a dangerous thing to do, because that area is so crowded. What if it fell down and hit someone?

 3

A: ¹(プライバシーの問題もあるよね). A drone in the city could be used to look into the windows of residences or businesses. Nonetheless, there are some really beneficial uses for civilian drones. One of them is in agriculture, where a drone can serve as a flying camera. They can "see" things that humans can't usually see.

B: ²((残念だけど) よく分からないわ).

A: In other words, the drone camera takes pictures of a huge field, one part at a time. It can tell how deep the green color is and tell the farmer which part needs more water or more fertilizer. ³(農家は問題を解決するための行動をすぐとれる).

B: That's pretty neat. ⁴(緊急事態のときにドローンができることにも感銘を受けたわ). For example, after a hurricane in the U.S., drones were used to find people who needed help. They also checked electricity lines in places emergency crews couldn't reach.

 4

A: ⁵(オーストラリアでの実に違った用途は海岸沿いの水域をパトロールすることだ) where people are swimming and surfing. These drones can spot sharks and notify lifeguards to get people out of the water in those areas.

B: There are lots of merits, but when drones are flown over people, ⁶(それらは落っこち

CHAPTER 1　Civilian Drones

て誰かを傷つけるかもしれない危険が常にあるのよね).
A: Well, engineers are working on that, experimenting with parachutes and cushioning. I think they'll come up with something that makes drones safer for everyday use.

Notes:
1 **operate**「操縦する、動かす」／ 7 **businesses** > business「会社、店」／ 13 **fertilizer**「肥料」／ 18 **spot**「見つける、監視する」／ 23 **come up with**「(答えなどを) 見つけだす」／ 23 **everyday**　形容詞なので注意。cf. every day

Try!

1 Dictation 🎧5
会話で日本語になっている部分の英語がもう一度ややゆっくりと話されるので書きとろう。

1 _____
2 _____
3 _____
4 _____
5 _____
6 _____

2 Vocabulary in Dictation
Dictation の文中に出てくる語句の使い方を覚えよう。
日本語の文は例文を参考にして英語にし、あとで英訳例の音声と比較してみよう。🎧6

❶ the issue of …

1. Let's try to solve *the issue of* part-time workers and contract workers.
2. *The issue of* taxes is one that politicians try to avoid whenever possible.
3. 多くの人たちが公然の場 (in public) でのプライバシーの問題について関心がある。

------

❷ I'm afraid I don't …

1. *I'm afraid I don't* understand what you mean.
2. *I'm afraid I don't* agree with your opinion.
3. 残念ですがあなたのパーティにいけないかもしれない。

CHAPTER 1   Civilian Drones

❸ take immediate action

1. The situation requires that we *take immediate action*.
2. The tragic accident underlines the need to *take immediate action*.
3. われわれが直ちに行動を起こさなければ、地球温暖化 (global warming) は急速に進むだろう。

---

❹ (be) impressed by …

1. *I'm impressed by* how he can deal with very irritating people.
2. Everyone in the audience *was impressed by* his powerful performance.
3. ほとんどの外国人訪問者は日本人のもてなし (hospitality) に感銘をうける。

---

❺ a different use

1. *A different use* of empty PET bottles is to store rice in them.
2. Overseas, *a different use* of Japanese noren is as a wall decoration.
3. 彼らはその土地の違った使いみちを市当局 (the city) に勧めた。

---

❻ the danger that …

1. Doctors should be more aware of *the danger that* patients will take unnecessary medicines.
2. Firefighters recognized *the danger that* the wind might increase the speed of the fire.
3. 休戦 (cease-fire) が破られる (break down) 危険があるだろうと新聞が言っている。

---

3 Comprehension Check

会話 🎧2-4 の内容についての次のそれぞれの英文を読んでその内容が正しければ T を間違いならば F をかっこの中に記入しよう。

1. The man who flew a drone over the crowd in Tokyo was caught by the police.   (   )
2. It is sometimes very helpful to use a drone for agriculture.   (   )
3. In Australia, drones are used to find missing people after a hurricane.   (   )

CHAPTER 1   Civilian Drones

Try more!

Partial Dictation 🎧 7

会話を聴いて空欄を埋めよう。(　　)内は単語が1語、点線部には数語入ります。

A: Last night I was watching a documentary about elephants in Africa and the images were fantastic. The filmmakers used drones to get up really ¹(　　) (　　) the animals.

B: Did the animals react to ²(　　) (　　) (　　) the drones?

A: They didn't seem bothered. Maybe the drones ³(　　) (　　) (　　).

B: I was impressed by a program I saw on birds and monkeys that live in the treetops of a jungle and never come down to the ground. The cameras on the drones easily followed them ⁴(　　) (　　) (　　) (　　), 20 meters or more up in the branches.

A: It's impressive to see even buildings, such as Buddhist temples and Shinto shrines, ⁵(.............................). Cameras in planes and helicopters can't get that close or stay steady for a long time.

B: Drones are ⁶(　　) (　　) (　　) for film and television crews. No doubt about it!

Questions for Discussion

1. Do you know any other uses for drones? What are they?

2. Should drone operators have to get a license? Why or why not?

3. Should the police be allowed to use drones in public places?

Chapter 2 Reading While Young

青春と読書

電車内で周囲を見回しても本を読んでいる人が誰もいないことがある。知識や情報はスマホから得られるかもしれないが、自分の頭で主体的に考える力を養うには読書がずいぶんと役に立つはずである。主体的に考え個を確立して生き抜く力を若いうちに身につけることができていれば、山あり谷ありの人生が待ち構えていても恐れるには足りないだろう。

Dialogue

まず会話を聴きましょう。日本語になっている部分の英語は印刷されていません。 8–10

A: People in completely different fields are warning that the rapid increase in screen time is having a negative impact on everyone these days. ¹(人はスマートフォンや他の電子機器 (and other electronic devices) にくぎ付けになっている (be glued to) ようだわ) from the time they wake up until they go to sleep at night.

B: ²(私は時代遅れのように聞こえるかもしれない), but I think they should spend less time online and more time reading. Looking at funny photos on an app and exchanging one-line messages with friends and acquaintances may seem interesting, but you can't learn from it and ³(それは考える機会を与えない). One of the most meaningful things I did when I was young was to read and think about what I had read.

A: Me, too. I would fall in love with a particular author and read every book she wrote. Then I'd find another author and do the same. I can still remember how much I enjoyed those books. And I learned about relationships and ⁴(物ごとを違った視点から見る方法).

B: I started out reading adventure stories and then moved on to histories and biographies. Sometimes ⁵(本に入り込みすぎて宿題をするのを忘れてしまった).

A: If a person doesn't read, how can he or she learn how to concentrate? If you can't stay focused on a story, an essay, or a newspaper article, you'll never be able to grasp ideas and to think critically. Electronic devices can provide material, but you don't really make a choice. You become a total consumer, not a thinking human being.

CHAPTER 2　Reading While Young

B: I believe that reading is particularly important for young people. Reading opens doors to other cultures, expands your knowledge, [6](そして人に重大な問題について考えるように促してくれる). If people don't read a lot, they won't learn to think for themselves. And they'll believe whatever appears in front of them on a screen.

Notes:
1– **screen time**　スマホやパソコンに関わっている時間のこと。／ 14 **start out**「取りかかる」／ 14 **move on to ...**「進む、進歩する、移る」／ 17 **stay focused on ...**「（関心などを）集中したままでいる」／ 19 **total consumer**「たんなる消費者」

Try!

1 Dictation 🎧 11

会話で日本語になっている部分の英語がもう一度ややゆっくりと話されるので書きとろう。

1 _____
2 _____
3 _____
4 _____
5 _____
6 _____

2 Vocabulary in Dictation

Dictation の文中に出てくる語句の使い方を覚えよう。
日本語の文は例文を参考にして英語にし、あとで英訳例の音声と比較してみよう。🎧 12

❶ be glued to ...

1. The little girl remained *glued to* her mother whenever they went out of the house.
2. His eyes *were glued to* the beautiful woman across the room.
3. 毎金曜の夜、私は好きなドラマを見ながらテレビにくぎづけになる。

_____

❷ behind the times

1. If you still use the term "word processor" you are *behind the times*.
2. Some bureaucrats are *behind the times* when it comes to not making information public.

CHAPTER 2 Reading While Young

3. 女性に対するその上司の態度 (attitude) は時代遅れだ。

---

❸ give (someone) a chance (to do something)

1. If you give her a chance to work, she might be a very good employee.
2. That three-day weekend gave me a chance to relax and wash clothes.
3. その留学プログラム (study-abroad program) は私のフランス語能力を伸ばす (improve) チャンスを与えてくれた。

---

❹ different points of view

1. When it comes to travel, my friends and I have different points of view.
2. In terms of the goals of education, there are many different points of view.
3. 日本人でない人 (non-Japanese) は多くの異なった視点から日本の文化をみる。

---

❺ get so into …

1. We got so into our discussion that we forgot we needed to catch our train.
2. It's risky to get so into SNS that you can't deal with people in person.
3. ジャックはマンガに入り込むあまりに日本へ移る (move to) ことを望んだ。

---

❻ challenge (someone) to (do something)

1. My new job challenges me to think about business in a new way.
2. My mentor's tough comments really challenged me to work harder.
3. アリスはテニスで競争しよう (compete against her) と私に挑んできた。

---

3 Comprehension Check

会話 🎧8-10 の内容についての次のそれぞれの英文を読んでその内容が正しければ T を間違いならば F をかっこの中に記入しよう。

1. People spend a lot of hours using electronic devices during the day.　　　(　)
2. Exchanging on-line messages with many people may give you a lot of knowledge.
　　　(　)
3. Young people should read more to develop their critical thinking.　　　(　)

CHAPTER 2   Reading While Young

Try more!

Partial Dictation 🎧 13

会話を聴いて空欄を埋めよう。(　) 内は単語が1語、点線部には数語入ります。

A: Have you finished reading that mystery you were raving about*?
B: No, but I'm ¹(　　　) (　　　　　) with it, and I can barely put it down*. I'll loan it to you as soon as I finish.
A: I'll give it a pass. I'm not that into mysteries ²(　　) (　　) (　　　) (　　　　), and I have a long list of books that I want to read. Next up is a ³(　　　　) (　　) about perceptions of time.
B: I guess our tastes don't overlap very much. But, to each his or her own*.
A: That's not necessarily the case. After all, we're both interested in mysteries—just different types of mysteries.
B: You've ⁴(.............................) there.
A: Why don't we agree to tell each other a two-minute summary of what ⁵(　　　　　) (　　) (　　).
B: *It's a deal!*

*rave about「夢中になって語る」/ *put down「本を読むのをやめる」/ *to each his or her own「人それぞれで」/ *It's a deal!「それがいい！」

Questions for Discussion

1. Is there a significant difference between how we read print books and ebooks?
2. Would you rather experience a story through a book, a manga, or a video?
3. Do you share what you read with other people?

Chapter 3: Intelligent Assistance

IAで!

AI (Artificial Intelligence)「人工知能」は恐ろしいほどの進化を遂げていて、IT (Information Technology) 社会を象徴する言葉になっている。しかし、現代人の生活はあまりに IT を頼りにし過ぎているのではないだろうか。スマホとも何もかも任せる一方的な依存関係ではなくて、便利な IA (Intelligent Assistance) としてほどほどの関係を保てると良いのだが。

Dialogue

まず会話を聴きましょう。日本語になっている部分の英語は印刷されていません。 14–16

A: Until I left my smartphone on the train one day, I didn't realize how dependent I was on it. It had my daily calendar, all of my contact addresses, my train pass and two years' worth of photos. ¹(それなしではほとんど何もできないかもしれないわ).

B: Were you able to get it back?

A: Fortunately, yes. Some kind person turned it in to the conductor on the train and he or she delivered it to the lost and found office. By the end of the day, I was able to go and pick it up.

B: ²(間一髪だったね). I've become a little cautious about putting too much information into my phone. Some people do their banking through their phone and use their phone to pay for things with electronic money. ³(なぜかそういうのは自分にはちょっと不安だな).

A: But it's so convenient. We don't have to carry cash and we can buy anything from a cup of coffee to jacket that we find on sale with it.

B: I guess I'm more interested in using the map function to help me find directions to a new place. And being able to check email during the day without carrying a laptop is really convenient.

A: ⁴(生活が大いに楽になるわよね)? One of my favorite uses for what I like to call my "personal assistant," that is, my phone, is to take images of important documents and handwritten notes with the camera. If I need some information quickly, I have it with me in one place.

B: ⁵(ソーシャルネットワークには積極的なの)？
A: No, that seems like a waste of time to me. I occasionally exchange messages with friends about meeting places and times, ⁶(でもそういったネットワーキングに私はあまり満足しないわ). I'd rather meet up and spend time talking in real life.

Notes:
3 **two years' worth of photos**「2年分の写真」／5 **turned it in** > turn ... in「…を渡す、提出する」／6 **lost and found office**「遺失物取扱所」／19– **I have it with me in one place**「私のひと所にある」スマホひとつで足りてしまうこと。／22 **occasionally**「ときたま、時どき」／24 **meet up**「出会う」

Try!

1 Dictation 🎧 17

会話で日本語になっている部分の英語がもう一度ややゆっくりと話されるので書きとろう。

1 _____
2 _____
3 _____
4 _____
5 _____
6 _____

2 Vocabulary in Dictation

Dictation の文中に出てくる語句の使い方を覚えよう。
日本語の文は例文を参考にして英語にし、あとで英訳例の音声と比較してみよう。🎧 18

❶ (can, could) hardly do anything without something

1. Brett *can hardly do anything without* his wife's approval.
2. When we travel abroad, we *can hardly do anything without* a dictionary.
3. 私は彼女の助言と支えがなければほとんど何もできないだろう。

_____

❷ a close call

1. On my way home, I had *a close call* with a bicyclist coming down the sidewalk.
2. The driver wasn't looking in my direction and it was *a close call*.

CHAPTER 3 Intelligent Assistance

3. 私たちは知床をハイキング中 (during our hike in Shiretoko) 熊と間一髪のところで助かった。

----

❸ make someone (a little, really) nervous

1. Not knowing the schedule for this week *makes* me *a little nervous*.
2. Having to give a presentation *makes* him *really nervous*.
3. 将来についての不確実さ (uncertainty) が私たちをちょっと不安にする。

----

❹ make life (a lot) easier

1. If buses came more frequently, it would *make life a lot easier*.
2. We all do what we can to *make* life *a little easier* for our grandparents.
3. コンピュータが生活を大いに楽にするかはよくわからないよ。

----

❺ active in

1. JICA* is *active in* building infrastructure in African countries.　　*国際協力機構
2. It's important to be *active in* some kind of volunteer service.
3. 彼女は 70 代 (in her 70s) だがまだ仕事に積極的だ。

----

❻ … is(n't) very satisfying to someone

1. Working nine to five at a boring job *isn't very satisfying to* most people.
2. Recently I find that reading history *is very satisfying to* me.
3. ギターを弾くのを習うことには私をとても満足している。

----

3 Comprehension Check

会話 🎧14–16 の内容についての次のそれぞれの英文を読んでその内容が正しければ T を間違いならば F をかっこの中に記入しよう。

1. One day the woman lost her smartphone and got it back the next day.　　(　)
2. Both of the speakers agree about the banking system on the phone.　　(　)
3. The man likes to use his phone as his secretary or assistant.　　(　)

CHAPTER 3　Intelligent Assistance

Try more!

Partial Dictation 🎧 19

会話を聴いて空欄を埋めよう。(　　) 内は単語が1語、点線部には数語入ります。

A: I bought a new smartphone last week and it's really neat!
B: Didn't you just buy a new one ¹(　　) (　　) (　　) (　　) (　　)?
A: Yes, but this one has a bigger screen, so I can even read books and newspapers on it. In the morning, I download the newspaper and ²(　　) (　　) (　　) on the subway coming into the city. If I don't have time to download that, I just continue reading a book I've started.
B: Has your ³(　　) (　　) gone up much?
A: Not really. The various providers have to be very competitive in order to keep customers, so I got a good deal. I'm now paying just ten percent ⁴(..), even with better service.
B: When I'm ready to upgrade my own phone, I'll have to get your advice.
A: I'm completely up to date on the best bargains, so just ⁵(..)!

Questions for Discussion

1. In your opinion, what is the biggest advantage of smartphones?

2. Are there any demerits of using a smartphone daily?

3. What kinds of "intelligent assistance" do you think we will see in the future?

Chapter 4: Keeping It Clean

リサイクルの大切さ

「ごみ箱」に「護美箱」と当て字をしているのを見かける。資源ごみはリサイクルすることによって、資源の節約だけでなく生物の命を含む地球の美を護ることにつながっている。今ではごみの分別収集は当たり前の時代になったが、道路の中央分離帯に捨てられている飲み物の缶やペットボトルも多い。ポイすてなどもっての外であることは言うまでもない。

Dialogue

まず会話を聴きましょう。日本語になっている部分の英語は印刷されていません。 20-22

A: Not too long ago, ¹(世間の人びとはリサイクルにそんなに努力しなかった). They didn't put newspapers and magazines in the right bins, but just threw them in the burnable trash bins. But it seems to me that people are making more of an effort to recycle, don't you think?

B: That may be, but I still see people dropping drink cans and plastic bottles along the sides of the roads. ²(誰かほかの人が彼らのゴミを拾わなければならないということを彼らは分かっていないようね), and it makes the neighborhood unpleasant to walk in.

A: The government, railways, and private companies have set out recycling bins for different items, including glass and cans, but ³(アメリカの故郷を思い出すよ) that there were different bins for clear glass and colored glass, and for steel cans and aluminum cans. Why don't Japanese do that, too?

B: Who knows? Maybe the government does the dividing after the recycling trucks haul them away.

A: They say that ⁴(アルミニウムはリサイクルしやすい) and that manufacturers are eager to buy up the supplies of recycled metal. I'd imagine that the same would be true for steel, but I'm not sure. I wonder about plastic drink bottles.

B: ⁵(プラスチックは沢山の損害を与えると科学者が言っているわ). It's especially a problem when it gets into the oceans. There are some gigantic swirls of plastic floating on the surface of the oceans off Hawaii. In other places, ⁶(プラスチックの小さな破片は分解して最後にそれを魚が食べる), thinking they are food. Those are the fish that may

CHAPTER 4　Keeping It Clean

end up on our dinner tables.
A: That is certainly an unpleasant thing to consider. Think of all the plastic bottles that are in a single vending machine along the street. I hope we don't end up eating pieces of them.

Notes:
3 **bin**「ごみ箱、ふた付きの大箱」／ 5 **plastic bottle**「ペットボトル」plastic はナイロン、ビニール、セルロイドなどのこと。／ 7 **walk in**「中にはいる」／ 13 **haul ... away**「…を運びさる」／ 15 **buy up**「買いあげる」／ 18 **gigantic swirls of plastic**「プラスチックの渦巻いている浮遊物」

Try!

1 Dictation 🎧 23

会話で日本語になっている部分の英語がもう一度ややゆっくりと話されるので書きとろう。

1 _____
2 _____
3 _____
4 _____
5 _____
6 _____

2 Vocabulary in Dictation

Dictation の文中に出てくる語句の使い方を覚えよう。
日本語の文は例文を参考にして英語にし、あとで英訳例の音声と比較してみよう。🎧 24

❶ make (too much of) an effort to...

1. Don't *make too much of an effort to* please that troublesome customer.
2. We should all *make an effort to* show up for appointments on time.
3. 私は自炊する (cook for oneself) 努力をしたためしがない。

_____

❷ (They) don't seem to realize (that) ...

1. They *don't seem to realize that* education is a great advantage.
2. Some politicians *don't seem to realize that* helping people get stable jobs is important.

CHAPTER 4　Keeping It Clean

3. 彼はその状況がどれだけ深刻か分かっていないようだ。

---

❸ back home

1. I was *back home* during the summer and enjoyed seeing old friends.
2. *Back home* in Mississippi, we eat a lot of corn bread and fried chicken.
3. 私は青森の故郷に帰った時には、その土地の方言 (local dialect) でしゃべる。

---

❹ (is) easy to …

1. This novel *is easy to* read and I highly recommend it.
2. Rice *is easy to* use in a wide variety of recipes.
3. その問題は彼にとっては解くのが簡単だった。

---

❺ do a lot of damage (to) …

1. Heavy trucks can *do a lot of damage to* highways.
2. Hurricane Irma did *a lot of damage to* the Texas coast.
3. そのスキャンダルはその俳優の評判を大いに傷つけた。

---

❻ end up (eat)ing

1. At most parties, I *end up eating* too much.
2. She'll *end up* in a fight if she keeps *talking* like that.
3. 彼女と私が音楽について意見を言い合う (discuss music) 時は、結局何時間も話すことになってしまう。

---

3 Comprehension Check

会話 🎧20-22 の内容についての次のそれぞれの英文を読んでその内容が正しければ T を間違いならば F をかっこの中に記入しよう。

1. These days people don't drop cans and bottles on the street. 　　(　)
2. According to the man, there are different recycling bins for steel cans and aluminum cans in the US. 　　(　)
3. The woman believes that plastic drink bottles are easy to recycle. 　　(　)

CHAPTER 4　Keeping It Clean

Try more!

Partial Dictation 🎧 25

会話を聴いて空欄を埋めよう。(　　) 内は単語が 1 語、点線部には数語入ります。

A: When I studied in the U.S., I participated in a community recycling project. We collected and sorted goods ¹(　　　) (　　　) (　　　) for several hours.

B: Who came up with that idea?

A: Several people in my neighborhood ²(　　　) (　　　) volunteers and a lot of exchange students signed up. We gathered clean used clothing on the first and third Saturdays and cans, bottles, and paper on the second and fourth Saturdays. We took the recyclable goods to a big central site, and we got ³(　　) (　　　) (　　) (　　) money for what we brought in.

B: How did the group use that money?

A: We bought ⁴(　　　) (　　) (　　　　　) to send to children in African village schools.

B: It sounds like your group was doing ⁵(.............................) at the same time.

A: Yes, and it made all of us feel like we were doing something really worthwhile.

Questions for Discussion

1. Have you become more careful about recycling in daily life?
2. Is there some way that plastic bottles can be reused?
3. Should consumers be taxed when they buy cans and bottles?

Chapter 5: Manners in Public

日本的美徳

「近頃の若者はマナーが悪い」とはもはや若者でなくなった元若者から耳にタコができるくらい聞かされる常套語である。交通機関の優先席に若者が老人をさしおいて座っている光景を見かけるのは目に余るほど多いわけではない。電車に乗っていると、マナーが悪くなっているのは若者に限らず日本人全体ではないかと強く感じる人は多いに違いない。

Dialogue

まず会話を聴きましょう。日本語になっている部分の英語は印刷されていません。 26–28

A: I only stayed in Japan for a week, but my impression of the Japanese was that they are extremely kind and polite.

B: That's basically true. But some Japanese complain that ¹(彼らと同じ市民がきちんとした感覚を失ってしまった) to act in public places. For example, on the subways, trains and buses, there are priority seats for the elderly, pregnant women and people with injuries.

A: I noticed those. ²(それらは他の国でも普通のことだわ), too.

B: The problem is that sometimes completely healthy passengers plop down in those seats and don't give them up to people who need to sit down. Sometimes these inconsiderate passengers pretend to sleep so they don't have to give up their seats.

A: ³(がっかりだわ). In a lot of countries, people will yield their seat regardless of whether it is a priority seat or not. It's a simple, kind thing to do.

B: I had one memorable encounter on the subway though. ⁴(毛を染めて耳と鼻にピアスの穴をあけた若者), and wearing really beat-up clothes was sitting down in the regular seats. When he looked up and saw an older woman slowly walk onto the train, he hopped up and offered his seat to her with a smile. I was reminded that ⁵(人は外見で判断できない).

A: One thing that did bother me a little was the smartphone zombies. Once, I was walking down the street with my suitcase, and guy coming the other way was so focused on his smartphone screen that he almost bumped into me. ⁶(私がどいてみ

CHAPTER 5　Manners in Public

たの), but he didn't look up, apologize or anything.

B: That's a problem even on subway platforms. That can be really dangerous, if someone ends up falling onto the tracks. I've even seen bicyclists checking their phones as they weave through pedestrians on the sidewalk. It's incredibly dangerous.

Notes:
5– **people with injuries**「けがをしている人」／ 10 **inconsiderate**「思いやりのない」＞ considerate ／ 10 **give up their seats**「彼らの席を譲る」／ 11 **yield**「与える、譲る」／ 14 **beat-up clothes**「おんぼろの洋服」／ 15 **walk onto the train**「電車に乗りこむ」／ 18 **smartphone zombies**「スマートフォンゾンビ」＝ people who seem 100% tied to their phone screens, with no sign of human sensitivity／ 24 **weave through ...**「…の間をじぐざぐに進む」

Try!

1 Dictation 🎧29

会話で日本語になっている部分の英語がもう一度ややゆっくりと話されるので書きとろう。

1. _____
2. _____
3. _____
4. _____
5. _____
6. _____

2 Vocabulary in Dictation

Dictation の文中に出てくる語句の使い方を覚えよう。
日本語の文は例文を参考にして英語にし、あとで英訳例の音声と比較してみよう。🎧30

❶ (lose) a sense of ...

1. Ron *lost* his *sense of* humor after his friend passed away.
2. It's important to have *a sense of* pride in your work.
3. 私は風邪をひいて味覚 (sense of taste) がなくなってしまった。

_____

CHAPTER 5   Manners in Public

❷ be common in …

1. Sushi restaurants *are common in* other countries around the world.
2. Unfortunately, populism *is common in* the U.S. and in other countries.
3. 近頃は、絵文字 (emoji) はよその国でもあたりまえだ。

---

❸ That's disappointing.

1. There are no concert tickets left? *That's disappointing*.
2. They never apologized for their rude comments. *That's disappointing*.
3. 君が金曜日の夜に加われない？　それは残念だ。

---

❹ a (young guy) with …

1. *An* older *guy with* no hair came into the café and ordered coffee.
2. *A young girl with* an expensive handbag sat next to me in the restaurant.
3. 顔に疲れた様子 (tired expression) がでているあの男 (guy) は私の友人のジムだ。

---

❺ judge people by …

1. It's wrong to *judge people by* their appearance alone.
2. I tend to *judge people by* how they speak to others.
3. 人をどのくらいお金を稼ぐ (earn) かで判断するべきではない。

---

❻ get out of the way

1. If we don't *get out of the way*, we'll block traffic*.　＊交通を妨げる。
2. If senior employees *get out of the way*, younger employees will advance.
3. 私はかろうじて (just in time) 対向車 (oncoming car) に道を譲った。

---

3 Comprehension Check

会話 🎧26–28 の内容についての次のそれぞれの英文を読んでその内容が正しければ T を間違いならば F をかっこの中に記入しよう。

1. There are also priority seats on the trains and busses in other countries.　　(　)
2. People sitting down in the regular seats don't have to yield their seats.　　(　)
3. It is very dangerous to look at a smartphone screen while walking on a platform.
　　(　)

CHAPTER 5　Manners in Public

Try more!

Partial Dictation 🎧 31

会話を聴いて空欄を埋めよう。(　) 内は単語が 1 語、点線部には数語入ります。

A: I come from the American South, where we talk about ¹(　　) (　　　) (　　)
(　　　　) and consideration for others. I think the Japanese are like that.

B: I agree. One of my favorite Japanese words is omoiyari, thoughtfulness for others
and ²(..).

A: Japanese also have an expression translated as "reading the air."

B: ³(　　) (　　) (　　) (　　)?

A: In English, kuki o yomu means "sense the mood" in a gathering. Nothing is
spoken, but you pick up on it. And you know ⁴(　　) (　　) (　　　　).

B: That's a unique expression. I'll have to add that to my vocabulary.

A: ⁵(..................................), but most people learn to do it.

Questions for Discussion

1. On average, how many minutes a day do you use a smartphone?

2. How often each day do you check SNS or text messages?

3. What are the benefits a smartphone provides?

Chapter 6 Which News Is Fake?

フェイクの見極め

フェイク (fake) とは「偽物」とか「ぺてん師」という意味だが、トランプ大統領登場のおかげでこの語が一般的になった。トランプ大統領は自分に都合が悪い情報やその情報を伝える新聞社などを fake とののしったが、インターネットで一方的な情報がその信ぴょう性を考えさせる間もなくあふれる現代社会の危険性はいつも頭に置いておくべきであろう。

Dialogue

まず会話を聴きましょう。日本語になっている部分の英語は印刷されていません。 32–34

A: When I was a kid, we used to get news from TV, radio, newspapers and news magazines. We pretty much believed what we read was true.

B: ¹(でも近頃はそうでないでしょう、ねえ)？

A: Definitely not. Now a lot of people get their news from social networks, blogs, twitter and a variety of websites. Sometimes they say things that are the complete opposite of each other.
By the time I got to college, I knew that The New York Times leaned toward the left and The Wall Street Journal leaned toward the right. I read both of them, and kept in mind that ²(それぞれが何を記事にしたかに傾向がある). I learned to be skeptical of both.

B: With internet and social network news, though, that's not so easy to do. It's hard to know who wrote the content and what they are trying to get us to believe.

A: We all know that politicians, business leaders, and commentators pick and choose facts and information to suit their needs. We learn not to believe everything they say one hundred percent. But when the president of the United States pointed at one journalist and said, "You're fake news!" ³(あれは度を越していたね), in my opinion.

B: I remember that. He refused to answer a question from that reporter.

A: Yes, and from my perspective, ⁴(それは危険な領域へ入る一線を越えた). The public has a right to ask questions, hear various points of view, and make its own decision about what to believe and what not to believe.

CHAPTER 6　Which News Is Fake?

 34

B: There is also the issue of how much information the public can demand. [5](秘密が守られてよいものを拡げようと努めている法律もあるのよ).

A: And businesses are already collecting information about us, where we live, what our faces look like, what we search for on the internet. All of this seems harmless for the moment, but [6](それはわたしたちのプライバシーに重大な影響をもっているかもしれないね). 25

Notes:
7 **lean toward ...** 「…の傾向がある」／ 8– **keep in mind**「心にとどめる」／ 9 **skeptical of ...**「…について疑う」／ 14 **suit ...**「…に適する、好都合である」

Try!

1 Dictation 🎧 35

会話で日本語になっている部分の英語がもう一度ややゆっくりと話されるので書きとろう。

1 _____
2 _____
3 _____
4 _____
5 _____
6 _____

2 Vocabulary in Dictation

Dictation の文中に出てくる語句の使い方を覚えよう。
日本語の文は例文を参考にして英語にし、あとで英訳例の音声と比較してみよう。🎧 36

❶ that's not the case

1. Working long hours used to lead to success, but *that's not the case* anymore.
2. Good quality clothing used to be expensive, but *that's not the case* anymore.
3. 彼は自分が家の実権を握っている (the boss at home) 思っている、しかし事実は違う。

_____

❷ slant on ...

1. Let's try a new *slant on* the current situation.

CHAPTER 6 Which News Is Fake?

2. The French *slant on* the EU is different from that of the Germans.
3. 彼は友人に話すことすべてに一つの傾向があった。

----

❸ go too far

1. In my view, his teasing *goes too far*.
2. Criticism of a poor person's appearance is *going too far*.
3. 昼食にハンバーグを3つも食べるのはまったく行き過ぎだ。

----

❹ cross a [the] line

1. Expecting his friend to pay for lunch is *crossing a line*.
2. His behavior at the party *crossed the line* between friendliness and rudeness.
3. その報告は事実と作りごと (fact and fiction) の間の境をこえている。

----

❺ keep secret

1. Let's *keep secret* what we know about his background.
2. They *kept secret* the fact that they were living together.
3. 彼は自分が正確には (exactly) 何歳であるかを秘密にしておくように言い張る (insist on)。

----

❻ have a serious impact on …

1. Events far away can *have a serious impact on* our own lives.
2. Automation will *have a serious impact on* job markets around the world.
3. 人口増加は環境に深刻な影響がある。

----

3 Comprehension Check

会話 🎧32-34 の内容についての次のそれぞれの英文を読んでその内容が正しければTを間違いならばFをかっこの中に記入しよう。

1. The newspapers used to have their own political tendencies.   (   )
2. We should accept what journalists say completely without questioning.   (   )
3. Our private information can be collected through our online research.   (   )

Try more!

Partial Dictation 🎧 37

会話を聴いて空欄を埋めよう。（　）内は単語が1語、点線部には数語入ります。

A: Do you often read any of the Japanese-language newspapers?
B: I confess that I don't read as much as I should, but I do ¹(　　　)(　　　) one of them at least twice a week. I try to rotate between the Asahi, Yomiuri, Nikkei, and Mainichi. Sometimes ²(　　　)(　　　)(　　　) and other times they are really different.
A: Each of them has a reputation for ³(　)(　　　)(　　　)(　)(　　　).
B: How do you get your news?
A: I have my tablet set to automatically download one paper to read on the subway. I occasionally buy another paper at a kiosk to get ⁴(..) on things.
B: ⁵(..), the electronic version or the actual paper version?
A: The electronic version is really convenient, but I still want a real newspaper to hold in my hands and read while I have ⁶(..).

Questions for Discussion

1. Which media do you use to learn about current events?
2. Are any social network media comparatively reliable? If so, which ones? If not, why not?
3. Is it possible to make news or information really neutral?

Chapter 7: Food Self-sufficiency

回復しない食料自給率

1989年に5割を割った日本の食料自給率は2009年には40パーセントになり、その後も4割に満たない時代が続いている。コメは100パーセントに近い自給率を保っている貴重な食料だが食生活の洋風化に伴いコメの消費量は減少する一方だ。「腹が減っては戦ができぬ」というならば、役人や政治家は輸入に頼る食料の面からまず安全保障を考えるべきだろう。

Dialogue

まず会話を聴きましょう。日本語になっている部分の英語は印刷されていません。 38–40

38

A: ¹(多くの日本人が有機 (organic) 野菜や有機果物を食べるのに熱心ね) and are opposed to genetically modified food. Frankly, Japan's low food self-sufficiency is more of a problem.

B: ²(君が問題だと思っているのは何かな)?

A: Japan currently only produces 37 percent of its own food. ³(それは下から2番目に低いわね) since Japan suffered a serious rice shortage in 1993.

B: What keeps this percentage so low? Is it because young people aren't taking up farming as the older generation retires?

A: That's bound to be one factor. But whenever there's cold weather during the growing season or a typhoon just prior to harvest, ⁴(お米の生産高に重大な低下があるのよ), wheat, potatoes and other crops, especially in Tohoku and Hokkaido.

 39

B: Are Japanese farmers actually producing enough rice to feed the entire country?

A: There is a high level of self-sufficiency in rice, but on the contrary, there's a drop in the annual per capita rice consumption. Currently, on average, ⁵(日本人（全体）は50年前に食べていた量の半分も食べていないわ).

B: I imagine that Japanese are eating more meat than they used to, right?

A: That's right. The country imports large quantities of pork, beef, and poultry meat. In terms of the value of imports, Japan is the largest meat-importing country in the world. The one bright spot is that domestic production of fruits and vegetables has gone up, so that has led to a decrease in imports, ⁶(少なくとも当分の間は).

CHAPTER 7 Food Self-sufficiency

B: I suppose that trade liberalization is a big issue for farmers, too.
A: Indeed, it is! And another long-term issue is the decline in domestic fishery product output. Saury and scallop catches are down, partly because large fishing fleets outside of Japan's Exclusive Economic Zone are taking large catches of fish before they can enter Japanese waters.

Notes:
2 **genetically modified food**「遺伝子組み換え食品」／ 7 **taking up** > take up「後を継ぐ」／ 9 **bound to be …**「～であるに違いない」／ 10 **prior to …**「～より前に」／ 14 **per capita**「一人当たり」／ 17 **poultry meat**「ニワトリなどの家禽の肉」／ 18 **in terms of the value**「重要性の面からみると」／ 23 **saury and scallop catches**「サンマとホタテ貝の漁獲高」／ 24 **Exclusive Economic Zone**「排他的経済水域」沿岸から 200 カイリ以内。

Try!

1 Dictation 🎧 41

会話で日本語になっている部分の英語がもう一度ややゆっくりと話されるので書きとろう。

1 _____
2 _____
3 _____
4 _____
5 _____
6 _____

2 Vocabulary in Dictation

Dictation の文中に出てくる語句の使い方を覚えよう。
日本語の文は例文を参考にして英語にし、あとで英訳例の音声と比較してみよう。🎧 42

❶ be eager to

1. We're all *eager to* meet our new manager.
2. I'm *eager to* start on my trip through Shikoku.
3. その日本の宿のスタッフは思いやりのあるマナーでお客に奉仕したいと希望している。

_____

❷ the issue as someone sees it

1. What's *the issue as* the French *see it*?

CHAPTER 7　Food Self-sufficiency

2. *The issue as* my coworkers and I *see it* is that we want time off.
3. 私の友人が問題だと思っているのは、日本の地下鉄は料金が高いということだ。

------

❸ the (second)-lowest level (since)…

1. The employment rate is at *the highest level since* the recession began.
2. Japan's university ranks are *the fourth-lowest since* 1990.
3. その大統領の人気は最近の歴史の中で最低の水準だ。

------

❹ a significant drop in …

1. There was *a significant drop in* consumer spending during the 1990s.
2. We felt *a significant drop in* temperature when the sun went down.
3. 日本の出生率はかなりの低下をしてきている。

------

❺ less than half of what …

1. *Less than half of what* Japanese eat is grown in Japan.
2. Some American workers earn *less than half of what* they did a decade ago.
3. 私のすることの半分も本当に楽しいことはない。

------

❻ for the time being

1. Let's forget about work *for the time being* and enjoy ourselves.
2. Let's leave the minor details aside *for the time being*.
3. 当分の間、彼女は両親に経済的に頼っている

------

3 Comprehension Check

会話 🎧38–40 の内容についての次のそれぞれの英文を読んでその内容が正しければ T を間違いならば F をかっこの中に記入しよう。

1. The recent percentage of Japan's food self-sufficiency is the lowest since 1993.　　　　　　　　　　　　　　　　　　　　　　　　　　　（　）
2. Imports of fruits and vegetables will increase for a while.　　（　）
3. Not only farming but also fisheries face long-term issues.　　（　）

CHAPTER 7　Food Self-sufficiency

Try more!

Partial Dictation 🎧 43

会話を聴いて空欄を埋めよう。(　　)内は単語が1語、点線部には数語入ります。

A: Before I came to Japan, I assumed that most Japanese ate traditional Japanese food ¹(　　) (　　) (　) (　　).

B: I sort of thought the same thing*. But from the movies I'd seen set in Japan, I knew that they had lots of Western fast-food shops.

A: Whatever they eat, they certainly stay slim. They ²(　　　) (　　) (　　　) a pretty balanced diet, except for the employees who eat just meat and rice for a cheap lunch.

B: What I really enjoy about Japan is that most meals are ³(　　) (　　　) (　) small portions of various ingredients. It looks good and it tastes good, too.

A: And ⁴(............................) that goes "hara hachibu," which literally means "fill your stomach only 80 percent full." ⁵(　　) (　　) (　　　), eat in moderation and don't overdo it.

B: Japanese cuisine is so delicious though. It's hard to refrain from ⁶(............................).

A: I guess you're hooked on Japanese food!

*I sort of thought the same thing.「ちょっと同じことを思っていた」

Questions for Discussion

1. Has your diet—what you eat regularly—changed since you were young?

2. Is food self-sufficiency really that important?

3. How can Japan realistically become more self-sufficient in food?

Chapter 8 Whose Fish?

やせるサンマ

魚は苦手という人でも全く魚を食べないという人は少ないだろう。日本人の食生活に魚は欠かせない。近年養殖物が増えたとはいえ、一年を通して日本人の食卓には魚がのぼる。サンマが出回りだせば、もう秋が来ると季節の移り変わりを人は感じるだろう。しかし、当たり前に食べられていた魚も資源の枯渇や漁獲を巡る激しい国際競争にさらされている。

Dialogue

まず会話を聴きましょう。日本語になっている部分の英語は印刷されていません。 44–46

A: ¹(最近新聞にたくさん載っているわ) about the decrease in the number of various kinds of fish around the world. According to the UN's most recent data, 32% of the world's fish stocks are being overexploited.

B: ²(これがこのまま続けば、一部の魚が食べられなくなってしまうよ) that we enjoy now.

A: That's true. ³(平均して、世界の人ひとりひとりは1年に20キロの魚を食べている). If overfishing occurs in areas close by, that means that fishermen have to go further away to catch fish.

B: And fishermen from every country in the world will compete to catch the same fish.

A: Each country has its own Exclusive Economic Zone, right?

B: Yes, but big commercial fishing boats can operate just outside of that 200 nautical-mile limit. That affects the number of fish closer to the coastline, too.

A: That means ⁴(ある種の魚をめぐって激しい奪い合いがある), but those fish don't "belong" to any particular country. So, ⁵(漁師は欲しいだけたくさん自由にとれる).

B: That's the current problem. They may take so many fish that the fish population cannot be sustained. That's a serious issue.

A: ⁶(このかなり先の見えにくい状況 (dim picture) の中にも二つの明るい点があるわ). One is the increase in farmed fish. Some fish can be raised in net-protected areas in natural bodies of water. Others can be raised at least partially in tanks on land. The second bright spot is a project being tried in New Zealand.

CHAPTER 8   Whose Fish?

B: What are they doing?
A: One local government made it illegal for anyone to catch any kind of fish within several miles of the coast. That allowed fish and the food they eat to grow safely in that area. The number of fish increased. When the fish swim out of that protected area, then fishermen are free to catch them. It's a win-win situation.
B: [7](もしどの国もがそうしたのなら、結果は本当に有益なものになるでしょう), right?

Notes:
3 **fish stocks**「漁獲量」stock(s)「総量」／ 3 **being overexploited**「過剰にとられている」exploit「（天然資源などを）開発する」／ 6 **in areas close by**「隣接した地域」／ 10 **Exclusive Economic Zone**「排他的経済水域」沿岸より 200 海里 (nautical-mile) 以内。／ 15 **population**「個体数」／ 25 **win-win**「双方が得をする」

Try!

1 Dictation 🎧47

会話で日本語になっている部分の英語がもう一度ややゆっくりと話されるので書きとろう。

1 _____
2 _____
3 _____
4 _____
5 _____
6 _____
7 _____

2 Vocabulary in Dictation

Dictation の文中に出てくる語句の使い方を覚えよう。
日本語の文は例文を参考にして英語にし、あとで英訳例の音声と比較してみよう。🎧48

❶ in the paper(s)

1. I read *in the paper* that X-Japan is going to have another concert!
2. It says *in the papers* he expects to win tournament.
3. この頃はノーベル文学賞のことが新聞にたくさん載っています。

_____

CHAPTER 8   Whose Fish?

❷ If this keeps up, …

1. *If this keeps up,* the rain will force us to cancel our trip this weekend.
2. *If this keeps up,* there won't be any land for people to live on.
3. もしこれがこのまま続くと、私たちはこの夏に休暇を取ることができないかもしれない。

---

❸ on average

1. I read, *on average*, about three books a week.
2. Young people, *on average*, don't get enough sleep at night.
3. 平均すれば、1週間を通じて私は600円を昼食に使う。

---

❹ (heavy) competition for …

1. Drug companies face *heavy competition for* a share of the market.
2. There's *heavy competition for* buyers in the smartphone industry.
3. ヨーロッパのサッカーチームはチャンピオンシップ・リーグをめぐっての激しい競争に立ち向かっている (face)。

---

❺ free to take (as much/many as they want)

1. Feel *free to take* as much time as you want.
2. My boss told me I'm *free to take* as many days off as I want to during this season.
3. バイキング式料理 (buffet) では食べたいだけの食べ物を自由にとれます。

---

❻ bright spots in … > bright spot (in, on)

1. My sister was the one *bright spot in* my family life.
2. There are a few *bright spots on* the economic horizon.
3. その交通事故におけるひとつの明るい点は誰も死者が出なかったことだ。

---

❼ be beneficial (to/for)

1. It's common knowledge that physical exercise *is beneficial for* health.
2. Sharing your feelings can *be beneficial to* building relationships.
3. 温泉は関節の痛みがある人 (people with aching joints) に効能があると考えられている。

CHAPTER 8   Whose Fish?

3 Comprehension Check

会話 🎧44-46 の内容についての次のそれぞれの英文を読んでその内容が正しければ T を間違いならば F をかっこの中に記入しよう。

1. The number of fish is decreasing because of overfishing.　　　( )
2. Fishermen from every country try to catch various kinds of fish.　　　( )
3. In New Zealand, it is illegal for anyone to catch any kind of fish near one local coast.　　　( )

Try more!

Partial Dictation 🎧49

会話を聴いて空欄を埋めよう。( ) 内は単語が 1 語、点線部には数語入ります。

A: Several of us are going to have sushi for lunch today. Would you like to ¹(　　　) (　　　)?
B: Sure, I'd enjoy that. I used to eat sushi regularly, but I've cut back* a little bit.
A: Well, prices ²(　　　) (　　　) (　　　), but nothing can beat sushi as a special treat.
B: The only problem with eating it for lunch, ³(.....................), is that we can't have sake or beer with it. That makes it even better!
A: That's true, but at least we can ⁴(.....................) the office and enjoy something different.
B: Agreed. What time ⁵(.....................) to head out*?
A: About 11:45. I'll let you know when we're ⁶(.....................).

*cut back「減らす」 *head out「出発する」

Questions for Discussion

1. How should fish quotas be decided between countries?
2. Are fish really in danger of being over-exploited?
3. Which countries eat the most fish?

Chapter 9: English: Necessary or Not?

英語必修論

英語教育の早期化を巡っては賛否両論がいまだあるが、「小学 3 年生からの必修化」「小学 5 年生からの教科化」が 2020 年度に完全実施されることになった。将来誰もが本当に英語が必要な職業に就くわけではないだろうが、英語を学ぶということは違う文化に触れる可能性が広がると言えることは間違いがない。

Dialogue

まず会話を聴きましょう。日本語になっている部分の英語は印刷されていません。 50–52

A: Why do you think it is that the Japanese government is promoting the study of English in the lower grades of school?

B: Leaders in the government feel that Japanese need to learn English in order to be competitive in the years to come. They think [1](それはネイティブスピーカーとの交渉にだけでなく不可欠だ), but also with speakers of other languages.

A: But it's always possible to use interpreters and translators, isn't it?

B: Yes, but leaders in various fields know that [2](起こっていることについていくためには彼らは英語が必要だ) in business, science, technology and even politics. Always depending on someone to translate for them leaves them [3](世界の他の国々の数歩後ろ).

A: I can see their point. But is it really necessary for every Japanese student to learn English?

B: I'm not sure. There's a large percentage of the population that will probably never need to use English, except when they travel abroad for a week or two. [4](彼らにとって時間の浪費のように見えるわね) to study so hard just to order in a restaurant in a foreign country.

A: To me, one of the usually overlooked values of learning English, or another foreign language, is learning a new way of thinking. It opens the door to other cultures. [5](それは競争やビジネスとは関係がないね).

B: It's also important to me because I can grasp another person's point of view and then explain my own ideas. Both sides can learn from that exchange.

CHAPTER 9   English: Necessary or Not?

A: That's true. When you try to explain your own country, you have to learn more about it. Learning English is just part of the preparation for real conversation with non-Japanese.

B: As I see it, [6](直接コミュニケーション出来るようになるということは間違いなく努力する価値がある). I'll continue learning for the rest of my life. And I'll enjoy doing it!

25

Notes:
1 **promote**「促進する」／2 **lower grades of school**「(小) 学校の低学年」日本の小学校 1 ～ 3 年。／16 **overlook**「見落とす、見のがす」

Try!

1 Dictation 🎧 53

会話で日本語になっている部分の英語がもう一度ややゆっくりと話されるので書きとろう。

1 _____
2 _____
3 _____
4 _____
5 _____
6 _____

2 Vocabulary in Dictation

Dictation の文中に出てくる語句の使い方を覚えよう。
日本語の文は例文を参考にして英語にし、あとで英訳例の音声と比較してみよう。🎧 54

❶ deal with (someone/something)

1. It's hard to *deal with* Adam when he's angry about something.
2. I'm trying to *deal with* my studies, my part-time job, and my club activities.
3. お客と対応するのは時には (occasionally) ストレスの多い (stressful) 体験です。

_____

❷ keep up with …

1. I *kept up with* her in the first part of the race, but she beat me to the finish line.
2. It's hard to *keep up with* what my friends are doing but I try to do it.

CHAPTER 9   English: Necessary or Not?

3. 技術の進歩 (technological advances) についていくのは本当に厳しいものだ。

------

❸ several steps behind [ahead]

1. However hard I work, I'm always *several steps behind* everyone else.
2. She's always *several steps ahead* in grasping new ideas.
3. 日本の福祉制度 (welfare system) は他の先進国のそれに比べて数歩遅れている。

------

❹ a waste of time

1. This new book on how to lose weight is *a* real *waste of time*.
2. Reading manga all the time is *a waste of time*, at least as I see it.
3. 政府のプロジェクトは時間の無駄と納税者 (taxpayers) のお金の無駄だった。

------

❺ have nothing to do with

1. I *have nothing to do with* her decision to quit her job and move to London.
2. My friends *have nothing to do with* the incident on the street.
3. 余暇の時間には (In my spare time)、私は仕事と関係のない何かをする。

------

❻ doing … is worth the effort

1. Learning a foreign language *is worth the effort*, definitely!
2. Exercising regularly *is worth the effort*, because I no longer have a sore back.
3. 私は料理が努力する価値があるかわからないので、外食しましょう (let's eat out)。

------

3 | Comprehension Check

会話 🎧50–52 の内容についての次のそれぞれの英文を読んでその内容が正しければ T を間違いならば F をかっこの中に記入しよう。

1. The Japanese government thinks that studying English is necessary to be competitive at school.　　　　　　　　　　　　　　　　　　　　　　　　　　　(　)
2. Most Japanese people will need to use English in business.　　　　　(　)
3. Learning English will help you communicate with people from different countries.
　　　　　　　　　　　　　　　　　　　　　　　　　　　　　　　　　　(　)

CHAPTER 9 English: Necessary or Not?

Try more!

Partial Dictation 🎧 55

会話を聴いて空欄を埋めよう。(　)内は単語が１語、点線部には数語入ります。

A: Do you think Japanese is a hard language to learn?
B: It's just as hard for me as English is for you. We have to make ¹(　　　) (　　　) (　　　) (　　) (　　　　　), just going in* the opposite direction.
A: I struggle with English pronunciation and idioms.
B: In reverse, Japanese pronunciation is comparatively easy. The hard parts are written characters and sentences that ²(　　　) (　　　) (　　) (　　　　　). It's hard to figure out who did what to whom.
A: Another tough part of English is all of the tenses. I ³(..................) about which one to use.
B: Studying all of the tenses before ⁴(　　　)(　　　) (　　) (　　　　　) to speak is probably not a great idea. Just learn the basic five or so, use them, then slowly add one more at a time.
A: That's quite different from ⁵(...) in high school!

*going in「内部に向かう」

Questions for Discussion

1. To you, what is the significance of learning English?
2. How is the best way to learn English or another foreign language?
3. In your opinion, is learning English essential for all young Japanese? Why or why not?

Chapter 10 Career Education

キャリア教育

大学生は4年間は勉強やサークル活動などの学生生活に打ち込める時間があるはずだがそれは理想にすぎないようだ。早い時期から準備しなくてはいけない就職活動のプレッシャーや労力は大変だろうが、就職のことを考える時に、自分の行きたい会社の社風や就きたい職種が自分の適性に本当に叶っているか考える余裕を持つことは大切なことであろう。

Dialogue

まず会話を聴きましょう。日本語になっている部分の英語は印刷されていません。 56–58

A: What are all those pamphlets you're looking at?

B: I just came back from the Career Center where [1](働く可能性のある所についての情報を集めて) and how to go about making applications. From friends who are a year or two ahead of me in school, I've been hearing about what a hassle job-hunting is. So, [2](まず第一歩を踏み出して出来るだけたくさんの情報を集めることにしたの).

A: I've heard from a lot of my Japanese classmates [3](彼らはそのことでとてもつらい時間を過ごしている).

B: It's draining to spend so much time doing that, when we need to be concentrating on our studies. Now I've found out that I should try internships at the companies I'm interested in. You go to a company for several days or a week and [4](その会社の社風を感じ取るために働くのね).

A: Wow, that's a really short time. In the States, students may spend two or three months during the summer as an intern at one company. Some of my American friends do one every summer until graduation. Several friends have gotten an offer from each company they interned with.

B: That's really different from our situation in Japan.

A: Another thing that's different. Some American students get an offer and then postpone starting to work. [5](彼らは仕事を始める前に1年の休暇を取って旅行に行くことがあるよ). Or they may teach in an economically-distressed school district for a year. Some end up liking the challenge of teaching so much that they turn down the

company offer and become full-time teachers.
B: That sounds really risky to me. Why do they do that?
A: Well, if your heart is in what you do, [6](安い給料しかもらえないかどうかは大した問題ではないさ).

Notes:
3 **go about**「とりかかる、始める」／ 3– **a year or two ahead of me in school**「学校で1年か2年上の」／ 4 **hassle**「厄介なこと、面倒なこと」／ 8 **draining**「消耗させる」／ 15 **each company they interned with**「彼らがインターンをしていたそれぞれの会社」／ 19 **economically-distressed school district**「経済的に困っている学校地域」／ 20 **end up liking …**「最後には…が好きになる」／ 23 **if your heart is in what you do**「自分のやることに熱意をこめられるのなら」

Try!

1 Dictation 🎧59

会話で日本語になっている部分の英語がもう一度ややゆっくりと話されるので書きとろう。

1 _____
2 _____
3 _____
4 _____
5 _____
6 _____

2 Vocabulary in Dictation

Dictation の文中に出てくる語句の使い方を覚えよう。
日本語の文は例文を参考にして英語にし、あとで英訳例の音声と比較してみよう。🎧60

❶ pick up information about …

1. Let's go by the Information Center and *pick up information about* this week's events.
2. I *picked up information about* her from various friends.
3. 休暇をとる前に (before taking a vacation)、私たちはフランスを旅することにについての情報を集める必要がある。

_____

CHAPTER 10   Career Education

❷ take the first step

1. Anne is *taking the first step* toward becoming a chemical engineer.
2. Next month my son will *take the first step* toward earning his own living.
3. ヴィンセントは芸術家になるという彼の大望の実現に向けての第一歩をついに踏み出した。

---

❸ have quite a hard time with …

1. We *have quite a hard time with* certain customers in our shop.
2. Our group is *having quite a hard time with* preparing our presentation.
3. 同僚と私は我われの上司と極めてつらい時間を過ごしている。

---

❹ get a feel for …

1. Ichiro quickly *got a feel for* how baseball is played in America.
2. I haven't *got a feel for* living in Japan yet, but I'm slowly learning.
3. 自炊する (cook one's own meals) コツをつかむまで長くかからなかった。

---

❺ take a year off

1. I plan to *take a year off* from university and study architecture in Italy.
2. Maria *took a year off* in order to devote herself to taking care of her baby.
3. 彼の先生は彼に絵を描く勉強のために1年の休暇をとるように奨励した。

---

❻ make (a lot of/little) difference (to someone) whether …

1. It *makes a lot of difference to* me *whether* I'm paid a fair salary.
2. It doesn't *make a lot of difference whether* we go today or tomorrow.
3. 私の約束が2時だったか3時だったかはほとんど問題ではない。

---

3 Comprehension Check

会話 🎧56–58 の内容についての次のそれぞれの英文を読んでその内容が正しければ T を間違いならば F をかっこの中に記入しよう。

1. It is really stressful for Japanese students to go job-hunting.　　　　(　)
2. Some Japanese students try to do an internship for a few months.　　(　)
3. American students need to start working soon after they graduate from college.
　　　　　　　　　　　　　　　　　　　　　　　　　　　　　　　　　(　)

CHAPTER 10 Career Education

Try more!

Partial Dictation 🎧61

会話を聴いて空欄を埋めよう。(　)内は単語が1語、点線部には数語入ります。

A: When did you begin looking for work?
B: When I was a freshman in university, I walked into the Career Services office one day ¹(　) (　) (　) what they suggested.
A: Freshman year? That was ²(　　　) (　　　), wasn't it?
B: Yes, but they did give me good information about what some companies look for. One thing was language skills, so I decided to study Japanese at university ³(　) (　) (　　　), then study in Japan for a year before graduating. Everything worked out* easily.
A: But what made you choose Japanese ⁴(　) (　) (　　　) (　　　)?
B: My family took in* ⁵(................................) from Sapporo when I was in junior high school. He became like a member of our family and I learned a lot about Japan from him. So, studying Japanese was something I'd always wanted to do.
A: You're working for a Japanese company now, so I guess the Career Services office ⁶(　) (　) (　) (　　　).
B: They sure did!

*work out「良い結果となる、うまくいく」 *take in「(客などを) 受け入れる」

Questions for Discussion

1. In order, what are the most important factor when choosing a place to work?
2. What can you learn from an internship?
3. How can you judge a company's atmosphere?

Chapter 11 Hours Worked

過重労働

長時間労働が深刻な社会問題化し「ノー残業デー」などを設ける会社も出てきた。しかし、仕事の量が同じなら結局どこかでノー残業の埋め合わせをすることになるのではと心配になる。ただ、効率の悪い働き方は仕事時間が増えて働く側にも会社側にもマイナスなので、働き方の見直しも必要だろう。勉強も時間より質が大切ということは言うまでもない。

Dialogue

まず会話を聴きましょう。日本語になっている部分の英語は印刷されていません。 62–64

A: The other day, I read an article in the newspaper about people who work for start-ups in San Francisco. ¹(それを読んでかなり唖然としたわ).

B: What did the article say?

A: Well, for one thing, it says the people who start these new ventures—and the majority are guys—just hustle all the time. ²(彼らは仕事以外のことは何もしないのよ). Some of them work 18 hours a day, and they say they're very happy.

B: ³(それじゃあ家族や旅行、あるいははどんな類のレジャーにも時間を取っておけないね). I've read that some big companies have 24-hour cafeterias in the company. They have showers, laundry service, and ATMs. That way, the employee never has to go home. To me that's insane.

A: Employees at some Japanese companies overwork. They put in 80 to 100 hours a month of overtime every month. How can they justify treating their workers like that?

B: Some critics say that a lot of those working hours are wasted. They say that many companies are just inefficient. The employees are in the office or out on sales calls, but they waste a lot of time. That's why they stay late, and ⁴(彼らはそうした時間に対して割増金を払ってもらえるんだよ).

A: Studies of businesses in Scandinavian countries show that employees are under pressure to get all of their work done within the regular working hours. It must be stressful, but ⁵(すくなくともたいていの日は彼らは時間通りに家に帰してもらえるわ).

CHAPTER 11   Hours Worked

B: There's one more, entirely different problem in Japan recently. It's that companies outsource jobs and hire only contract workers. Workers who are part-time or contract employees don't get all of the benefits that full-time workers do.

A: And ⁶(彼らは生計を立てるのに十分な時間を得ることを心配しなければならないわ). I don't know which is worse: working too much or not working enough.

Notes:

1– **start-up**「(おもに IT 関連の) 新興企業」／ 5 **just hustle all the time**「まあ一日中ハッスルしている」／ 10 **insane**「正気でない」／ 11 **put in**「費やす」／ 15 **inefficient**「能率的でない」／ 15– **sales call**「セールス訪問」／ 18 **Scandinavian countries**「スカンディナヴィア諸国」ノルウェイ・スウェーデン・デンマークに、時にアイスランドとフィンランドを含める。／ 22 **outsource**「外注する」／ 23 **contract worker**「契約社員」

Try!

1 Dictation 🎧65

会話で日本語になっている部分の英語がもう一度ややゆっくりと話されるので書きとろう。

1 _____
2 _____
3 _____
4 _____
5 _____
6 _____

2 Vocabulary in Dictation

Dictation の文中に出てくる語句の使い方を覚えよう。
日本語の文は例文を参考にして英語にし、あとで英訳例の音声と比較してみよう。🎧66

❶ be stunned by …

1. I *was stunned by* the news that she was leaving her job and getting married.
2. The world *was stunned by* the news of the assassination.
3. 私たちはどのくらいの仕事をしなくてはいけないのか聞いた時には茫然とした。

_____

❷ do something besides …

1. Can't you *do something besides* criticize me all the time?

CHAPTER 11 Hours Worked

2. Let's *do something besides* the regular routine on Saturday.
3. 私は月曜日から金曜日まで仕事のほかにはなにもしない。

---

❸ leave time for something

1. During our trip to the hot spring, we *left time for* a visit to a pottery shop.
2. Sandra *leaves time for* some exercise on every business trip she takes.
3. 赤ちゃんの世話は多くの仕事のための時間を残さない。

---

❹ get paid extra for …

1. Bill doesn't *get paid for* all of those late hours he puts in at work.
2. She's happy to work late because she *gets paid extra for* everything over 42 hours per week.
3. 法律は従業員が午後6時以降に働くことに対して割増賃金を支払われるよう求めている (require)。

---

❺ on time

1. I make it a rule to pay all of my bills *on time*.
2. She had to pull an all-nighter* to get her term paper done *on time*. *徹夜をする。
3. 飛行機が定刻通りなら、私たちは3時半までにパリに到着する (get to) でしょう。

---

❻ earn a living

1. That old guy *earns a living* by writing mysteries set in* ancient Venice. *舞台にしている。
2. It seems to most people that she is just too lazy to *earn a living*.
3. ヴィンセントは芸術家として生計を立てるのは容易でないことが分かった (found)。

---

3 Comprehension Check

会話 🎧62-64 の内容についての次のそれぞれの英文を読んでその内容が正しければTを間違いならばFをかっこの中に記入しよう。

1. Most Japanese employees work more than 100 hours of overtime a month. (　)
2. People who work overtime may actually waste a lot of time. (　)
3. Contract workers are employed on equal terms with full-time workers. (　)

CHAPTER 11　Hours Worked

Try more!

Partial Dictation 🎧 67

会話を聴いて空欄を埋めよう。(　) 内は単語が 1 語、点線部には数語入ります。

A: How are things going at work?
B: Oh, I can't complain. I'm usually able to get away* by 6:00 and go by the gym ¹(　)(　)(　)(　　). How are things with you?
A: Really busy. I just ²(　　)(　　　　)(　) assistant manager, and there's a sharp learning curve*. Every day I have to check on* the people ³(　　)(　　) (　　　　) to see if work is progressing according to schedule.
B: Well, congrats* on your promotion! I hope that means you got a raise, too.
A: Not a big raise, but enough to treat you to lunch. ⁴(.........................) at 12 noon on Thursday?
B: You bet*? I'll ⁵(...............................).
A: Okay, meet you at MacDonald's at 12:00!

*get away「抜け出す」 *learning curve「学習曲線」 *check on「確認する」 *congrats「おめでとう」= congratulations　* You bet?「きっとか？」

Questions for Discussion

1. How many hours do you think the workweek should be? Why?
2. Would you prefer to work at your own pace and stay late, or push hard and go home early?
3. Do you think that most Japanese companies are efficient or inefficient

Chapter 12: Gender Equality

ジェンダー・ギャップ

生物学的には男と女の数はほぼ半々で平等になっているが、職場や家庭といった社会的な場では男の優位が保たれているのは厳然たる事実だろう。世界経済フォーラム (WEF) が女性の地位を経済、教育、政治、健康の4分野で分析し、毎年発表する「世界の男女平等ランキング」の2017年版では日本は調査対象144カ国のうち114位と過去最低となった。

Dialogue

まず会話を聴きましょう。日本語になっている部分の英語は印刷されていません。 68-70

A: [1](男女平等といえば), it seems to me that Japan is way behind the times. The government talks about making it easier for women to work, but there isn't much progress.

B: [2](状況は以前よりは良いわ), but it's still hard to work and have children. If there were enough childcare facilities for little children, mothers would be able to go back to work after maternity leave.

A: Occasionally I see businesswomen and businessmen dressed for work with their young children. It looks like they are going to drop off their kids on the way to the office. [3](男性がそういうことをするのを以前はあまり見かけなかったね), but now I do. That's a defi- nite improvement.

B: I've noticed that, too, and [4](育児休暇 (paternity leave) をとっている父親の割合はわずかね).

A: But a lot more needs to be done, especially inside the companies. [5](女性のCEO (最高責任者) は大きな注目を得るようだ), but in most companies, there is still a glass ceiling. Few women get promoted to the top positions. There is still a gap between men and women in the upper ranks.

B: The other day when I was watching the news on TV, they showed members of a local government committee seated around a meeting room. There must have been 50 members in the group, but only 3 women. That's hardly equality. So it's not just the private sector.

A: America has some of the same problems, especially in start-ups and the IT businesses. [6](職場の多くは男性優位 (male-dominated) だね) and many women feel like

CHAPTER 12　Gender Equality

they don't get the respect and the promotions that they deserve.

B: How do the Scandinavian countries score so high in terms of gender equality? Does the educational system somehow support equal treatment? Does the government support daycare for children of working parents?

A: [7](官と民の多くのやり方を結びつけているというのが僕の見方だ).　25

Notes:

4 **childcare facilities**「託児施設」facilities 通常複数形で「便宜（を図るためのもの）、施設、設備」／ 5 **maternity leave**「産休、母親の育児休暇」cf. paternal leave ／ 7 **drop off**「（車などから）降ろす」／ 11 **CEO**「最高経営責任者」Chief Executive Officer ／ 12– **glass ceiling**「ガラスの天井」管理職などへの昇進を阻む目には見えない特に女性に対する性的偏見。／ 18 **private sector**「経済界総体の民間部門」public sector（公共部門）とともに経済界の全体を構成する。／ 19 **start-ups**「（おもにIT関連の）新興企業」(Chapter14 に start-ups) ／ 22 **score** ここは動詞。

Try!

1 Dictation 🎧71

会話で日本語になっている部分の英語がもう一度ややゆっくりと話されるので書きとろう。

1 _____
2 _____
3 _____
4 _____
5 _____
6 _____
7 _____

2 Vocabulary in Dictation

Dictation の文中に出てくる語句の使い方を覚えよう。
日本語の文は例文を参考にして英語にし、あとで英訳例の音声と比較してみよう。🎧72

❶ When it comes to …

1. *When it comes to* mountain climbing, count me out.
2. *When it comes to* fresh fish, Tsukiji is fantastic.
3. コンピューターのことと言ったら、太郎は何でもできる。

_____

CHAPTER 12　Gender Equality

❷ be better (or worse etc.) than (it) used to be …

1. Karen's Japanese ability *is better than it used to be*.
2. Relations between the two nations *are worse than they used to be*.
3. 税金が以前より高くなった。

----

❸ didn't use to do …

1. I *didn't use to* get up until 9:00 in the morning.
2. She *didn't use to* exercise much at all.
3. あなたは以前も東京に住んでいませんでしたか？

----

❹ take (paternity) leave

1. One of our employees is *taking* maternity *leave* beginning next month.
2. Alice *took* sick *leave* to recuperate* from her injury.　＊回復する。
3. なぜもっと多くの男性が育児休暇 をとらないのだろうか？

----

❺ (get) (a lot of) attention

1. Apple *gets a lot of attention* when it puts out a new smartphone.
2. My puppy *gets a lot of attention* when we go for a walk.
3. その２国間の関係はメディアの多くの関心 (attention) をひいた。

----

❻ (male)-dominated

1. Government bureaus tend to be *male-dominated* workplaces.
2. *Female-dominated* professions tend to suffer from lower pay.
3. IT 関連の新興事業 (IT start-ups) は若者優位の業務 (businesses) になる傾向がある。

----

❼ My understanding is that …

1. *My understanding is that* we are supposed to meet on Monday at 3:00.
2. *My understanding is that* the company will replace all of the defective machines.
3. 学校はすべての学生に適切な値段で (at a reasonable price) 昼食を用意する (provide) ようにというのが私たちの見解だ。

CHAPTER 12　Gender Equality

3 Comprehension Check

会話 68-70 の内容についての次のそれぞれの英文を読んでその内容が正しければ T を間違いならば F をかっこの中に記入しよう。

1. It has become much easier for women to work and raise children in Japan.　(　)
2. A glass ceiling means an invisible barrier preventing women from promotion in a company.　(　)
3. Even America cannot be called a gender-equal society.　(　)

Try more!

Partial Dictation　73

会話を聴いて空欄を埋めよう。(　) 内は単語が 1 語、点線部には数語入ります。

A: Didn't you once tell me that your mother worked until you went to college?
B: Yes, my parents were divorced, so she had to work to support us. She continued until ¹(　) (　　　　) (　　　　) and she remarried.
A: It's hard enough for women now, but it must have been harder ²(　) (　　　) (　　　　).
B: It was. She often complained about how none of her bosses knew ³(................................) and she had to do their work for them. After I met a few of them, I realized she was telling the truth. Eventually she became the boss ⁴(　) (　) (　　　).
A: Did she go college first?
B: She ⁵(　　　) (　　) (　　　) at college, but didn't study, so she dropped out. Then she worked until she got married and had me.
A: She ⁶(................................) "career path," didn't she?

Questions for Discussion

1. Is the government capable of guaranteeing gender equality?
2. Are men and women capable of doing all types of jobs? Why or why not?
3. Can university education promote gender equality? If so, how?

Chapter 13   Where Does the Stress Come From?

ストレスはどこから？

ストレスと言ってもその原因となる要素は騒音や暑さ寒さ、過労などから人間関係などの社会的な要因まで様々ある。この章では労働時間の長さや休日の日数などがストレスとどのように関係するのか外国の例なども引き合いに出しながらの会話のやり取りを聴いてみよう。ストレスの要因は単純ではないと思うとまたストレスがたまるかも知れない。

Dialogue

まず会話を聴きましょう。日本語になっている部分の英語は印刷されていません。 74–76

A: What's wrong?
B: Oh, my neck and shoulder muscles are all tight. ¹(ぜんぶ職場でかかっているストレスのせいに違いないわ). I can't think of any other cause. There's a lot of work to be done and we don't have enough people to do it.
A: ²(ストレスは日本では共通の話題のようだね), among every age group.
B: It must be because Japanese work such long hours.

A: Actually, according to a lot of recent research, Japanese no longer work more than everyone else. Times have changed. The country that works the most hours per year is surprisingly Mexico. Mexicans work about 2,250 hours a year. The South Koreans work more than 2,100 hours a year, and the Japanese are somewhere over 1,700.
B: So, ³(日本人が世界で一番（労働に）時間を費やしているんじゃないの). That's surprising. I thought they did!
A: No. Even the Americans work longer hours than the Japanese nowadays, at a little less than 1,800 hours per year.

B: ⁴(休日の日数に違いがあるのかしら) the people in each country get. You know, ⁵(それは彼らがストレスをどれだけ感じるかに影響するのかもしれないわ).
A: Well, Japan only gets 15 paid holiday days per year, compared to 30 for both France and Finland.
B: Then, do the French and the Finns have less stress?

CHAPTER 13　Where Does the Stress Come From?

A: No, for them, it's less work but more stress. Ironically, Japanese workers put in more hours on working, but seem to have less stress than those in both of those countries.
B: Why is that?
A: It seems that [6](労働時間の短い国はストレス関連の病気が多い傾向がある). It may be that when people work shorter hours they have more time to worry about things. I'm not sure but that's just my take on the situation.

Notes:
20 **Finns**「フィンランド人」the Finns「フィンランド国民」cf. Finnish ／ 27 **someone's take on something**「〜についての…の見解」

Try!

1 Dictation 🎧 77

会話で日本語になっている部分の英語がもう一度ややゆっくりと話されるので書きとろう。

1 _____
2 _____
3 _____
4 _____
5 _____
6 _____

2 Vocabulary in Dictation 🎧 78

Dictation の文中に出てくる語句の使い方を覚えよう。
日本語の文は例文を参考にして英語にし、あとで英訳例の音声と比較してみよう。 🎧 78

❶ It must be … (with a noun or an adjective)

1. *It must be* the pollen* that is making me sneeze.　＊花粉
2. It must be the loud music that is giving me a headache.
3. イタリアをぐるりと旅する (travel around) のは素敵にちがいない。

_____

❷ a common subject

1. Finding a daycare center is *a common subject* in young families.

CHAPTER 13 Where Does the Stress Come From?

2. Yesterday's soccer game is *a common subject* during lunch in the cafeteria.
3. 職探し (job-hunting) は大学生の間の共通の話題だ。

---

❸ put in hours

1. She *puts in* several *hours* at her office on Saturdays, too.
2. If you *put in* a lot of *hours* on practicing, you'll slowly improve.
3. 私は自分のプレゼンテーションに備えて 10 時間を費やした。

---

❹ I wonder if …

1. *I wonder if* this plan will work out.
2. *I wonder if* the trains are running on time.
3. 彼女は私たちのキャプテンになるのに最適なチームメイトなのだろうか。

---

❺ have an effect on

1. What she said *had a* powerful *effect on* my decision to study abroad.
2. His encouragement *had an* enduring *effect on* my career.
3. そのニュースは週末に向けての私たちの旅行計画に影響があった。

---

❻ tend to…

1. I *tend to* work better when I'm under pressure.
2. My father *tends to* have a lot of work at the end of every month.
3. 人は宗教について語るのを避ける傾向がある。

---

3 Comprehension Check

会話 74–76 の内容についての次のそれぞれの英文を読んでその内容が正しければ T を間違いならば F をかっこの中に記入しよう。

1. The woman has stiff shoulders because of hard work.   (   )
2. The Japanese used to work longer than the Americans.   (   )
3. The French have less stress because they get more paid holidays.   (   )

CHAPTER 13　Where Does the Stress Come From?

Try more!

Partial Dictation 🎧79

会話を聴いて空欄を埋めよう。(　　)内は単語が１語、点線部には数語入ります。

A: What do you do to relieve stress?
B: I regularly take long walks in quiet parts of the city. When I have a few minutes during the day, I do stretching exercises. Sitting at a desk is one of ¹(　　)(　　) (　　) your body can do, you know.
A: I know, but a lot of what I do forces me to sit, either in meetings or ²(　　) (　　) (　　) a laptop keyboard.
B: If at all possible, try to stand up at least ³(　　) (　　) (　　), stretch your legs, and make circles with your arms, backward and forward.
A: Is there ⁴(　　) (　　) that I can do that's simple?
B: Definitely get off one or two stops early when you commute to work or to your home. Walking one stop gives your heart some exercise, and you get a ⁵(................................), too.
A: Sounds like good advice. I'll give it a try.

Questions for Discussion

1. Do you ever feel you are under stress? If so, when?
2. How does stress affect people? Is stress always bad for them?
3. In general, do you think that Japan is a stressful country to live i

Chapter 14: The Age of Childlessness

少子化時代の覚悟

少子化がこのまま続くと日本の人口は 2065 年には 8800 万人に減るという。人口減の深刻さはもっぱら経済成長や年金制度の維持の面から語られることが多い。しかし、女性の出生率を高めるための対策には限界があるだろう。人口が減っていくのは社会が成熟し、男でも女でも多様な生き方を選択できるようになった証しだとする覚悟が必要かもしれない。

Dialogue

まず会話を聴きましょう。日本語になっている部分の英語は印刷されていません。 80–82

A: It's often pointed out that Japan has an increasingly lower birthrate and an increasingly higher life expectancy rate. If things continue this way, there'll be few young people to take care of a large number of older people.

B: [1](みんなはそれを進行中の危機としてみているわ). With fewer young people working and paying taxes, what will happen to pensions and medical payments? Recently, however, [2](違った見方が出されてきているの). This view is that childlessness is not necessarily a problem.

A: What do you mean?

B: According to this view, the baby booms in the second half of the 20th century were a kind of blip in birthrates. Until then, a lot of people stayed unmarried because they couldn't set up households of their own for one reason or another. Many never married or had children.

A: So, in a way, [3](子供のいないことって第 2 次世界大戦の前には普通だったことへの回帰なの)?

B: Yes. Currently, there are varied, overlapping reasons why people do not have children. Some can't find the right person to marry. Some marry divorced people who already have children. Some put their careers first and postpone having children. But actually, childless people tend to be slightly happier than parents.

A: That's a significant factor. What makes them happier?

B: [4](ある人は子供を教えることに自分たちのエネルギーを注ぐわ). Some get involved in

CHAPTER 14　The Age of Childlessness

community activities like daycare centers, coaching youth sports teams, or after-school tutoring programs. One woman has started a charity called Bread and Books, which helps children mostly in Africa. Others may do things with nieces and nephews and children who have lost their parents in accidents.

A: ⁵(ある子供のいない人たちが慈善事業を始めたとどこかで読んだなあ). They support the charity with time and money when they are alive ⁶(そして後は遺言で慈善事業にお金を残すんだ).

B: Perhaps childlessness is more of a life choice than I thought it was.

Notes:
1 **point out**「（事実などを）指摘する」／ 2 **life expectancy rate**「平均余命」／ 2 **If things continue this way**「事態がこのように続くと」things のさまざまな用法に注意。cf. I have a lots of things to do today. ／ 5 **pension**「年金」／ 9 **the second half of the 20th century**「20 世紀の後半」cf. first half of the third inning「3 回の表」／ 10 **blip**「一時的な異常」／ 15 **overlapping reasons**「重複する理由」／ 20 **get involved in ...**「…と関わる」

Try!

1 Dictation 🎧83

会話で日本語になっている部分の英語がもう一度ややゆっくりと話されるので書きとろう。

1 _____
2 _____
3 _____
4 _____
5 _____
6 _____

2 Vocabulary in Dictation

Dictation の文中に出てくる語句の使い方を覚えよう。
日本語の文は例文を参考にして英語にし、あとで英訳例の音声と比較してみよう。🎧84

❶ ... in the making

1. Paying low wages to workers is a crisis *in the making*.
2. The crowd attended the race, hoping to see history *in the making*.
3. 急な山の斜面 (steep mountainsides) に家を建てるのは進行中の危機です。

_____

55

CHAPTER 14   The Age of Childlessness

❷ put forth

1. Journalists *put forth* a flurry of questions about the government's plans.
2. No one has *put forth* a workable plan to solve the traffic congestion.
3. 新しい競技場のデザインがもう一人の建築家 (architect) から提出された。

---

❸ a return to …

1. Thoreau, Rousseau, and other intellectuals called for *a return to* nature.
2. It will be hard for countries in the Mid East to make *a return to* prewar conditions.
3. 訓練によって (with practice)、彼は昔の体型 (old form) に戻ることに成功した。

---

❹ throw one's energy into …

1. I believe in my work, so I *throw all my energy into* it.
2. More women are *throwing their energies into* their careers.
3. 彼は自分のしている総てのことに膨大な量の (enormous amount of) エネルギーを注いでいます。

---

❺ read (hear/see/*etc*) somewhere that …

1. I recently *read somewhere that* the batteries in electric cars are improving rapidly.
2. I *saw somewhere that* Bright Electronics is offering a 10% discount this week.
3. 私の友人は列車が台風のために (due to the typhoon) 遅れているとどこかで聞いた。

---

❻ in one's will

1. He provided for his children *in his will*.
2. *In her will*, she left a large bequest to the university she graduated from.
3. 彼女の叔父は遺言により多額の (a large sum of) お金と家を彼女に残した。

---

3 Comprehension Check

会話 🎧 80–82 の内容についての次のそれぞれの英文を読んでその内容が正しければ T を間違いならば F をかっこの中に記入しよう。

1. A newly presented view on childlessness will solve the low birthrate problem. (   )
2. There were several reasons why many people didn't marry or have children before World War II.   (   )
3. Some childless people take part in a variety of social activities with pleasure. (   )

CHAPTER 14 The Age of Childlessness

Try more!

Partial Dictation 🎧 85

会話を聴いて空欄を埋めよう。(　)内は単語が1語、点線部には数語入ります。

A: Didn't you mention once that you have lots of brothers and sisters?
B: Yes, my father remarried and I have three half-brothers* and three half-sisters. They're a great bunch* and we really enjoy ¹(　　　) (　　　) (　　　).
A: Do you have lots of ²(......................................), too?
B: Only four. Three of my siblings* are unmarried. One has three kids and one has only one child.
A: ³(......................................)?
B: I don't know what usual is. My grandmother had seven brothers and sisters. My mother was an only child, and I'm an only child. ⁴(......................................)?
A: ⁵(......................................) and that's all. He can't find a girlfriend and I can't find an appealing boyfriend, so who knows how our lives will turn out*.

*half-brother「異母（異父）兄弟」 *bunch「仲間、連中」 *sibling「（男女の別なく）きょうだい」
*turn out「〜になる」

Questions for Discussion

1. In your view, does Japanese society expect people to have children?
2. What will happen if Japan's population decreases?
3. Can government policies encourage people to have children? How? Or why

Chapter 15 Less Romance in Japan

ロマン不在時代？

学生時代に将来の結婚について考える者は少ないだろう。結婚なんて遠い先のことに思えて当たり前である。最近は恋愛さえ面倒だとクールに敬遠する若者も増えていると聞くが、本当に人を好きになってしまえばそんなに冷静になれるはずはない。ただ、いろいろなことに縛られる結婚という制度には疑問を持つ男女が増えていくのは確かなことだと言える。

Dialogue

まず会話を聴きましょう。日本語になっている部分の英語は印刷されていません。 86–88

A: ¹(20代と30代の多くの日本人の女友達は) don't seem to be particularly interested in going out on dates with guys. When I ask why, they often say that they can't find any interesting guys or that all of the attractive guys are already married.

B: But I've also read that a lot of single Japanese women are happy without boyfriend or husband. ²(彼女たちは自活するのに十分なお金を稼ぐ) and they think that being married would be a hassle. I wonder if that's really true.

A: From what my friends tell me that's true. They work hard all day, but they can eat out or buy something to take home for supper. ³(彼女たちは別の人の都合に合わせる必要がないのよ).

B: Most of the single guys that I know say they'd like to get married, because they don't want to cook for themselves or clean house. It almost sounds as if they are more interested in having a maid than a partner.

A: If that's all they want, then ⁴(女性が結婚にしりごみをするのも不思議ではないわ). However, that doesn't necessarily mean that they don't want to have children. Some want to have children, but not a husband.

B: I don't know what the situation is in Japan, but in the States, there has been a slow increase in the number of people of each age who have never had a romantic relationship.

A: It's not just that kind of relationship. ⁵(それはただ友人とつきあうだけということに当てはまるわね). People spend a lot of time online, checking social networks and sending

CHAPTER 15 Less Romance in Japan

text messages, but they feel uncomfortable in face-to-face conversations. They would rather send a message than even talk on the phone.

B: There's something unsettling about all that.

Notes:

2 **going out on dates** > go out on a date 「デートに出かける」／ 6 **hassle**「厄介なこと、面倒なこと」／ 7– **eat out**「外食する」／ 23 **unsettling**「人騒がせな、混乱させるような」

Try!

1 Dictation 🎧89

会話で日本語になっている部分の英語がもう一度ややゆっくりと話されるので書きとろう。

1 _____
2 _____
3 _____
4 _____
5 _____

2 Vocabulary in Dictation

Dictation の文中に出てくる語句の使い方を覚えよう。

日本語の文は例文を参考にして英語にし、あとで英訳例の音声と比較してみよう。🎧90

❶ in one's (20)s

1. My friends in their 40s are beginning to buy their own houses.
2. All of her friends in their teens have their own mobile phones.
3. ボブは 40 代に見える、しかし実際は (actually) 60 だ。

_____

❷ earn money to live

1. Can I earn enough money to live in London as a designer?
2. Together* the couple earns enough money to live in a house.   *協力して。
3. 彼女はすでに自活するのに十分なお金を稼いでいる。

_____

CHAPTER 15 Less Romance in Japan

❸ adjust to someone's schedule

1. I'll be happy to *adjust to your schedule* when you are in Japan.
2. Sales staff try to *adjust to their customers' schedule* in making calls.
3. もしあなたが私の都合に合わせてくれることができるのなら、私は本当に感謝するのだが。

---

❹ shy away from something or someone

1. He *shies away from* girls because he doesn't know how to talk with them.
2. One of my bad habits is to *shy away from* making decisions.
3. その会社は全責任をとる (accept full responsibility) のを避けようとした。

---

❺ hang out with someone

1. On weekends, I like to *hang out with* friends at the beach.
2. *Hang out with* the wrong crowd and you could get into trouble.
3. 私は高校時代からの友人二人と一日つきあって過ごした。

---

3 Comprehension Check

会話 🎧86–88 の内容についての次のそれぞれの英文を読んでその内容が正しければ T を間違いならば F をかっこの中に記入しよう。

1. Young Japanese women mostly enjoy their single life without boyfriends and husbands. (　　)
2. Some single guys are not interested in getting married at all. (　　)
3. People should spend more time online to find a partner. (　　)

Try more!

Partial Dictation 🎧 91

会話を聴いて空欄を埋めよう。(　)内は単語が1語、点線部には数語入ります。

A: When I'm with people who speak English, I often don't know what to talk about.
B: Well, what do you talk about with Japanese who you meet ¹(.....................)?
A: That's different. I rarely meet a Japanese person who is ²(　) (　　　　) (　　　　). When we meet, someone introduces us. I know something about them ³(　) (　) (　　　　).
B: You can always talk about the weather. That's a safe subject. Or you can ask what kind of work the other person does. Then you can find out whether they live in Japan or whether they have traveled in Japan. ⁴(　　) (　　) (　　) (　) (　　).
A: I guess I'm also anxious about making mistakes in English.
B: That's ⁵(.....................). Mistakes aren't that important. The other person will appreciate the effort you are making to communicate.
A: Maybe I shouldn't be too self-conscious.
B: Everyone likes to ⁶(.....................), so give it a go*.

*give it a go「試してごらん」

Questions for Discussion

1. Would you rather spend time alone or do something with friends?
2. In your opinion, is having a boyfriend or girlfriend important?
3. Is it possible to have a career and a family?

自習用音声について

本書の音声は以下より無料でダウンロードできます。
予習、復習にご利用ください。

http://www.otowatsurumi.com/3845

上記 URL をブラウザのアドレスバーに直接入力して下さい。
パソコンでのご利用をお勧めします。圧縮ファイル (zip) ですので
スマートフォンでの場合は事前に解凍アプリをご用意下さい。

Listening to Dialogues on Social Issues
〈社会的な問題についての会話リスニング15章〉

編著者	James M. Vardaman
	野 地　薫
発行者	山 口 隆 史

発　行　所　　㈱音羽書房鶴見書店
〒113-0033　東京都文京区本郷 3-26-13
TEL 03-3814-0491
FAX 03-3814-9250
URL: https://www.otowatsurumi.com
e-mail: info@otowatsurumi.com

2018年 3 月 1 日　　初版発行
2023年 3 月15日　　4 刷発行

Copyright © 2018 by James M. Vardaman

組版　ほんのしろ／装幀　吉成美佐（オセロ）
印刷・製本　㈱シナノ
■ 落丁・乱丁本はお取り替えいたします。　　EC-069